FEEL THE LOVE WITH

# VOWS FROM THE HEART

## YOUR STEP-BY-STEP GUIDE TO WRITING MEANINGFUL WEDDING VOWS

WRITTEN BY: KAYLA RUH

ASSISTED WITH AI

# TABLE OF CONTENTS

# What are wedding vows?

**Definition and historical background.**

Wedding vows are promises made by each partner to the other during a marriage ceremony. These vows typically include commitments of love, fidelity, and support, and they serve as the foundation for the couple's life together. While the specific wording and structure of vows can vary greatly, their central purpose remains the same: to articulate the couple's devotion and intentions for their marriage.

## CHAPTER 01

The tradition of exchanging vows dates back centuries and varies significantly across cultures and religions. In ancient Roman times, marriage vows were straightforward, involving a mutual agreement and a handshake. As Christianity spread, the church began to formalize marriage ceremonies, incorporating vows as a key component. Medieval Christian ceremonies often included vows of fidelity and support, which laid the groundwork for the more elaborate promises we see today.

In many Western cultures, traditional vows often stem from the Book of Common Prayer, first published in 1549. These vows typically included promises to love, cherish, and honor one another "till death do us part."

Over time, as societal norms evolved, so too did the language and content of wedding vows, reflecting changing views on marriage, gender roles, and personal expression.

## Different cultural perspectives on wedding vows:

**Western Traditions**

In many Western countries, wedding vows are often personalized to reflect the unique relationship between the couple. While some couples choose to write their own vows, others may opt for traditional vows provided by their religious or secular officiant. These vows often emphasize love, support, and a lifelong commitment.

## Hindu Traditions

In Hindu weddings, the vows, known as "Saptapadi" or "Seven Steps," are a significant part of the ceremony. The couple takes seven steps around a sacred fire, with each step representing a promise or vow, such as nurturing each other, growing together in strength, and remaining friends and partners for life. These vows emphasize mutual respect, fidelity, and the well-being of the family.

## Jewish Traditions

Jewish wedding vows, known as "Sheva Brachot" or "Seven Blessings," are recited under the chuppah (wedding canopy). These blessings, recited in Hebrew, praise God, celebrate the couple's joy, and ask for blessings on their marriage. The vows often include a promise to love, honor, and cherish one another, reflecting the sanctity and commitment of the marital bond.

## Muslim Traditions

In Islamic weddings, the vows, known as "Nikah," are a contract between the bride and groom, often with the presence of witnesses. The couple may exchange promises to fulfill their marital duties according to Islamic law. The vows emphasize mutual respect, support, and the importance of a harmonious family life.

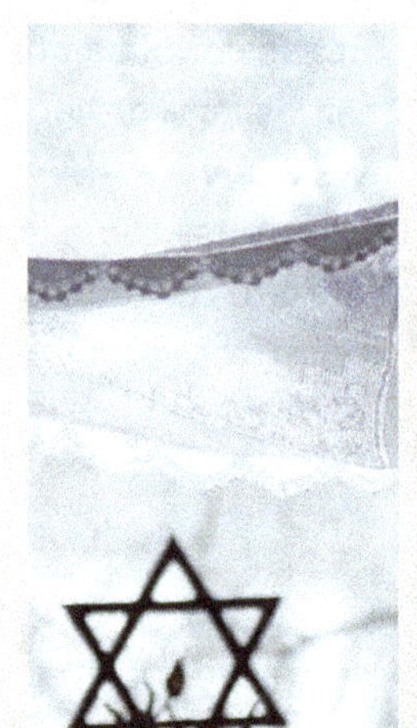

## Buddhist Traditions

In Buddhist weddings, the vows may include promises to support each other's spiritual journey and to live together in harmony. These vows often focus on compassion, mindfulness, and the shared commitment to lead a life that reduces suffering and increases happiness.

## African Traditions

African wedding ceremonies are rich with diverse traditions and customs. In some cultures, vows are exchanged in the form of proverbs or symbolic actions rather than spoken promises. These vows often emphasize community, family, and the continuity of cultural heritage, highlighting the couple's role in maintaining and strengthening these bonds.

Understanding the historical background and cultural diversity of wedding vows provides a deeper appreciation for their significance. Whether you choose to follow a traditional path or create your own personalized vows, this rich tapestry of traditions can inspire you to craft vows that resonate with your unique love story and shared future.

# Why vows matter?

The Emotional Impact on You and Your Partner.

### A Deep Personal Connection

Wedding vows are more than just words; they are a profound expression of your love and commitment to your partner. As you stand before each other and declare your promises, you are articulating your deepest emotions and intentions. This moment solidifies the bond between you, reinforcing the love and dedication that have brought you to this significant day. By openly expressing your feelings, you create a deeper emotional connection, laying a strong foundation for your future together.

### A Promise of Support and Partnership

The vows you exchange are not only declarations of love but also commitments to support and stand by each other through life's challenges and triumphs. This mutual promise of support fosters a sense of security and partnership, reassuring both you and your partner that you are not alone in facing whatever the future holds.

The act of making these promises aloud reinforces your commitment to work together and support each other, no matter what obstacles you may encounter.

### A Moment of Reflection and Gratitude

Writing and sharing your vows allows you to reflect on your relationship and express gratitude for the journey you've shared. This reflection can deepen your appreciation for each other and the unique bond you share. It's a moment to acknowledge the growth and experiences that have brought you together and to look forward with hope and excitement to the future you will build together.

# The Significance to Your Families and Guests

## A Public Declaration

Your wedding vows are a public declaration of your love and commitment, shared in front of your family and friends. This moment allows your loved ones to witness and celebrate the depth of your bond. By sharing your vows with your guests, you are inviting them to be a part of your love story, creating a communal experience that strengthens the connections between you, your partner, and your community.

## A Symbol of Unity

For families and guests, your vows symbolize the unity and merging of two families. This moment represents not only the joining of two individuals but also the creation of new relationships and bonds between your families and friends. It's a time for everyone present to come together in support of your union, fostering a sense of community and shared joy.

## Inspiration and Affirmation

Hearing your heartfelt vows can be an inspiring and affirming experience for your guests. Your words may remind them of the power of love and the importance of commitment, reigniting their own feelings and commitments in their relationships. This shared emotional experience can strengthen the bonds within your community and create lasting memories for everyone present.

Wedding vows are a crucial element of the marriage ceremony, serving as a profound expression of love, commitment, and mutual support. The emotional impact of these vows on you and your partner can deepen your connection and strengthen your partnership. For your families and guests, your vows represent a public declaration of your love, a symbol of unity, and an inspiring affirmation of the power of commitment. By understanding the importance of wedding vows, you can approach this pivotal moment with the depth and sincerity it deserves, creating a meaningful and lasting foundation for your marriage.

# The Promise of a Lifetime

How Vows Symbolize Commitment and Love

### A Sacred Pledge

Wedding vows are one of the most sacred and significant promises you will make in your lifetime. They symbolize the deep commitment and unwavering love you have for your partner. By speaking these vows, you are publicly affirming your intention to remain devoted and supportive, regardless of the challenges life may bring. This act of making solemn promises serves as a powerful testament to your dedication and loyalty.

### Personal and Unique

While traditional vows provide a timeless foundation, many couples choose to write their own vows to reflect their unique relationship. Personalized vows allow you to include specific promises and sentiments that are meaningful to you and your partner. This personal touch makes the vows even more special, as they are tailored to the nuances of your relationship and the experiences you have shared together.

### Expressions of Deep Emotion

The words spoken during your vows are a direct reflection of your innermost feelings and the love you share. They encapsulate the unique bond you have formed with your partner and convey the depth of your emotions. Vows often include promises of love, respect, and care, capturing the essence of your relationship and your commitment to nurture it. This expression of love is not just for the moment but is intended to endure for a lifetime.

# Vows as a Foundation for Your Marriage

## Building Blocks of a Strong Relationship

Wedding vows lay the groundwork for a successful and enduring marriage. They establish a mutual understanding of the promises and commitments that will guide your relationship. By clearly articulating your intentions and expectations, you create a strong foundation based on trust, respect, and shared values. These vows become the building blocks that support and sustain your marriage over time.

## Guidance in Difficult Times

Marriage inevitably comes with its share of challenges and obstacles. Your wedding vows serve as a guiding light during these difficult times, reminding you of the promises you made to each other. When faced with adversity, reflecting on your vows can provide strength and motivation to work through issues together. The commitments you made on your wedding day can help you navigate conflicts and reaffirm your dedication to each other.

## A Source of Inspiration and Renewal

Throughout your marriage, revisiting your vows can be a source of inspiration and renewal. Whether on anniversaries or during significant life events, reflecting on your promises can reignite the passion and love that brought you together. This practice can help you maintain a strong connection and continuously reinforce the foundation of your relationship. By periodically reaffirming your vows, you can keep the spirit of your wedding day alive and vibrant.

### Creating a Legacy

The vows you make on your wedding day are not only a promise to each other but also a legacy for future generations. They set an example of commitment and love for your children, family, and friends. Your dedication to upholding your vows can inspire those around you and contribute to a culture of strong, loving relationships. In this way, your vows extend beyond your marriage, influencing and enriching the lives of those who witness your union.

Wedding vows are more than just words; they are a profound and enduring promise of love and commitment. By symbolizing your dedication to each other, your vows lay the foundation for a strong, resilient marriage. They provide guidance during challenging times, serve as a source of inspiration, and create a legacy of love for future generations. Embracing the significance of your vows can help you build a marriage that is rooted in trust, respect, and unwavering devotion, ensuring a lifetime of shared happiness and fulfillment.

# ADDITIONAL TIPS...

**Reflect on the Journey You've Shared**

### Celebrate Your Story

Before you start writing your vows, take time to reflect on the unique journey you and your partner have shared. Consider the milestones, adventures, and challenges that have brought you closer. Reflecting on your shared history can help you identify the key moments that have shaped your relationship and the qualities in your partner that you cherish most. By celebrating your story, you can create vows that honor the past and highlight the special bond you share.

### Personal Anecdotes

Incorporating personal anecdotes into your vows can make them more meaningful and relatable. Think about the moments that define your relationship – your first date, a memorable trip, or a time when your partner supported you through a difficult situation. These stories can illustrate the depth of your connection and bring your vows to life, making them uniquely yours.

### Lessons Learned

Reflecting on your journey together also means acknowledging the lessons you've learned along the way. Consider how your relationship has helped you grow as individuals and as a couple. Sharing these insights in your vows can show your partner how much you value the experiences you've shared and how they have strengthened your bond.

### Think About Your Future Together

#### Shared Dreams and Goals

As you write your vows, envision the future you want to build together. Think about your shared dreams, goals, and aspirations. Whether it's starting a family, traveling the world, or pursuing a mutual passion, including these visions in your vows can convey your commitment to creating a fulfilling future together. By focusing on what lies ahead, you emphasize your dedication to growing and evolving as a couple.

#### Commitment to Growth

Marriage is a journey of continuous growth and change. In your vows, express your commitment to supporting each other's personal and mutual development. This could include promises to encourage your partner's dreams, to be patient during challenging times, and to celebrate each other's achievements. By acknowledging the importance of growth, you set the stage for a dynamic and resilient partnership.

#### Building a Life Together

Consider the everyday aspects of building a life together. Your vows can include promises related to the daily acts of love and support that strengthen your relationship. Whether it's cooking dinner together, sharing responsibilities, or simply being there for each other, these commitments show that you are ready to embrace the joys and challenges of married life.

#### Don't Stress About Perfection; Focus on Sincerity

#### Authenticity Over Perfection

Your vows don't need to be perfect; they need to be sincere. Rather than striving for eloquence or poetic flair, focus on speaking from the heart. Authenticity resonates more deeply than polished prose. Let your true feelings and emotions guide your words, ensuring that your vows reflect your genuine love and commitment.

### Embrace Vulnerability

It's okay to show vulnerability in your vows. Sharing your true emotions and even your fears can make your vows more relatable and heartfelt. Vulnerability fosters intimacy and connection, showing your partner that you trust them with your deepest feelings. This openness can strengthen the emotional bond between you and your partner.

### Keep It Simple

Sometimes, simplicity is the key to sincerity. You don't need to use elaborate language or grandiose promises. Clear, straightforward expressions of love and commitment can be just as powerful. By keeping your vows simple and to the point, you ensure that your message is clear and heartfelt.

### Practice, But Stay Present

Practicing your vows can help you feel more comfortable and confident when it's time to deliver them. However, don't worry if you stumble or forget a word during the ceremony. Staying present in the moment and maintaining eye contact with your partner is far more important. Your sincerity and the emotions you convey will resonate more than perfect delivery.

Writing your wedding vows is a deeply personal and meaningful task. By reflecting on the journey you've shared, thinking about your future together, and focusing on sincerity over perfection, you can craft vows that truly capture the essence of your love and commitment. Remember, your vows are a promise of a lifetime, so let them be an authentic reflection of your unique bond and the beautiful future you envision together.

# Getting Started: Preparation and Planning

**Setting the Scene**



## CHAPTER 02

### When to start Thinking About Your Vows

Writing your wedding vows is a significant and personal task that deserves ample time and thought. Starting the process early ensures that you can reflect deeply and create vows that genuinely capture your feelings and commitments. Here's a guideline on when to begin:

### 6-12 Months Before the Wedding

This is an ideal time to start thinking about your vows. At this stage, you're likely more relaxed and can take your time to reflect on your relationship without the immediate pressure of the wedding day. Begin by discussing with your partner if you'll write your vows together or separately, and if you'll follow traditional vows or create personalized ones.

### 4-6 Months Before the Wedding

By this point, you should begin gathering your thoughts and inspiration. Consider what elements are important to include in your vows, such as personal anecdotes, promises, and shared dreams. Start jotting down ideas and significant memories that you might want to include.

### 2-3 Months Before the Wedding

Start drafting your vows. Writing early allows you to let your thoughts evolve and mature. Don't worry about getting it perfect on the first try; this is the time for creativity and exploration. Share drafts with a trusted friend or family member for feedback if you feel comfortable.

### 1-2 Months Before the Wedding

Begin revising and refining your vows. Ensure they convey your emotions clearly and authentically. Practice reading them aloud to check for flow and length. Make sure your vows complement each other if you and your partner are writing separately.

### 2-4 Weeks Before the Wedding

Finalize your vows. At this stage, your vows should be polished and well-rehearsed. Write or print them out neatly to have a clean copy for the ceremony. If you're prone to nerves, consider having a backup copy for your officiant or a close friend.

# Creating a Timeline for Writing and Revising

## Step-by-Step Timeline

### 6-12 Months Before: Initial Discussions and Inspirations

### 4-6 Months Before: Initial Brainstorming

- **Discuss:** Talk with your partner about the type of vows you want.
- **Inspiration:** Start gathering inspiration from books, movies, and other weddings.
- **Brainstorm:** Begin brainstorming ideas and jotting down important memories.
- **Outline:** Create a rough outline of what you want to include.

### 2-3 Months Before: First Draft

- **Draft:** Write the first draft of your vows.
- **Review:** Read through it and note areas for improvement.

### 1-2 Months Before: Revision and Refinement

- **Revise:** Make revisions to enhance clarity and emotional impact.
- **Practice:** Start practicing reading your vows aloud.

### 2-4 Weeks Before: Finalization and Rehearsal

- **Finalize:** Complete the final version of your vows.
- **Backup:** Prepare a clean copy and consider having a backup.

### 1 Week Before: Final Practice

- **Rehearse:** Do a final rehearsal to ensure you're comfortable with your vows.
- **Relax:** Take a deep breath and relax, knowing you're prepared.

# Additional Tips for Setting the Scene

### Create a Dedicated Space

Find a quiet and comfortable place to work on your vows. This space should be free from distractions, allowing you to focus on your thoughts and feelings. Whether it's a cozy corner at home, a favorite park, or a quiet café, choose a place where you feel inspired and at ease.

### Set the Mood

Surround yourself with items that inspire you, such as photos of you and your partner, sentimental objects, or your favorite music. Setting the mood can help evoke the emotions and memories that will make your vows special.

### Stay Organized

Keep all your notes and drafts in one place, whether it's a notebook, a digital document, or an app. Staying organized will make it easier to track your progress and make revisions as needed.

### Be Patient and Kind to Yourself

Writing your vows is an emotional and sometimes challenging process. Be patient with yourself and allow time for writer's block or moments of doubt. Remember, this is a labor of love, and your efforts will be worth it when you stand before your partner on your wedding day.

Choosing the right time to start thinking about and writing your wedding vows is crucial for crafting meaningful and heartfelt promises. By creating a thoughtful timeline and setting the scene for inspiration and reflection, you can ensure your vows are a true reflection of your love and commitment. Take your time, be patient with yourself, and remember that sincerity and authenticity are key to creating vows that will resonate for a lifetime.

# Finding Inspiration


Sources of Inspiration

Books, Movies, Poetry, and Real-Life Stories

Drawing inspiration from various sources can help you craft wedding vows that are heartfelt, meaningful, and uniquely yours. Here are some ideas to get you started:

Books

Books are a treasure trove of beautiful language and profound insights about love. Look to classic literature, romance novels, or even non-fiction books about relationships for inspiration. Some notable examples include:

- **"Pride and Prejudice" by Jane Austen**
  - Known for its eloquent expressions of love and the journey of understanding and acceptance.
- **"The Notebook" by Nicholas Sparks**
  - A modern love story filled with emotion and memorable quotes
- **"The Velveteen Rabbit" by Margery Williams**
  - Offers touching insights into love and what it means to be truly loved.

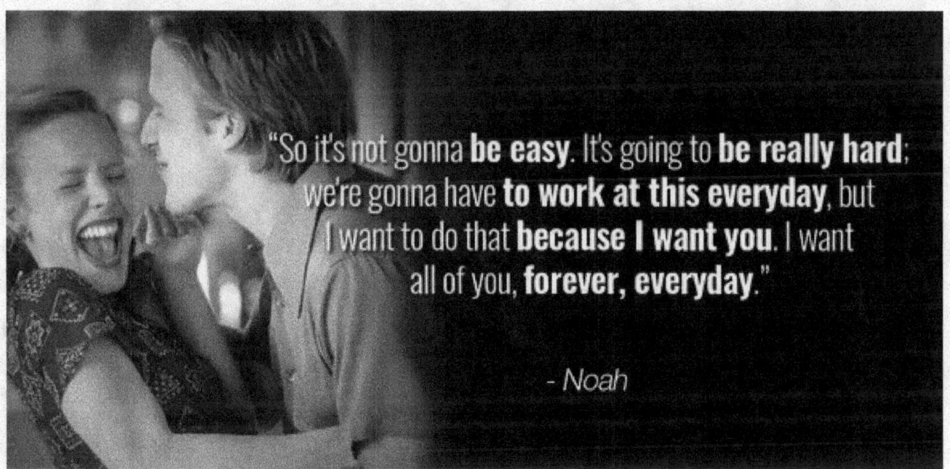

Movies often encapsulate the essence of love through memorable dialogues and scenes. Consider the following films for inspiration:

- **"When Harry Met Sally"**
  - Known for its realistic and touching portrayal of love and friendship.
- **"The Princess Bride"**
  - Filled with iconic lines and fairy-tale depiction of true love.
- **"Eternal Sunshine of the Spotless Mind"**
  - Offers a unique and thought-provoking perspective on love and memory.

Poetry distills emotions into concise and powerful language, making it a rich source of inspiration for your vows. Consider works by poets such as:

- **Rumi**
  - His poems explore deep and spiritual aspects of love.
- **Pablo Neruda**
  - Known for passionate and evocative love poems.
- **E.E. Cummings**
  - Offers a modern and whimsical take on love and relationships.

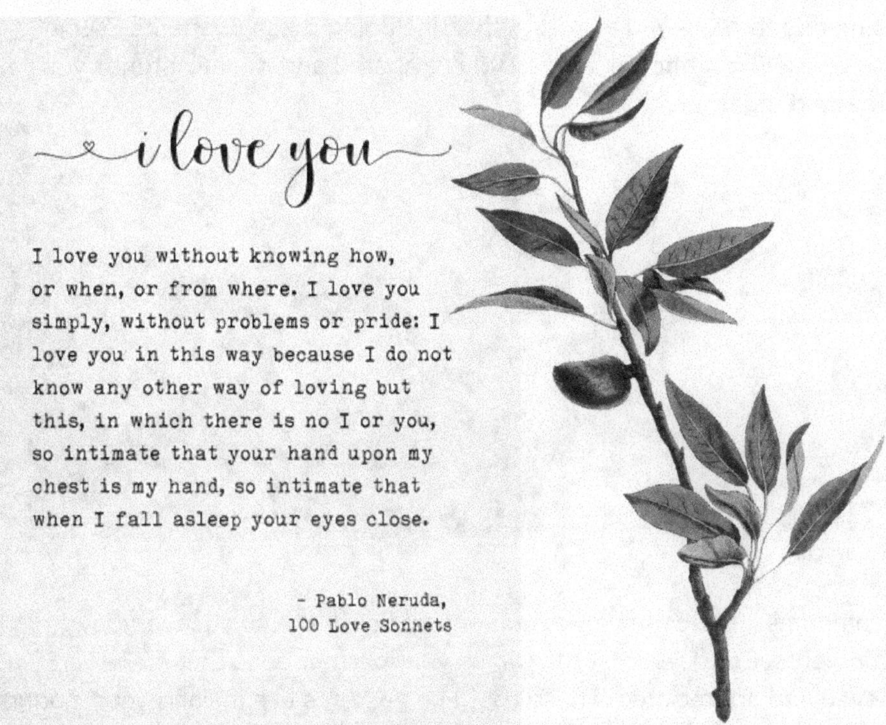


## Real-Life Stories

Sometimes the most inspiring love stories are those of real people. Look to the relationships of family and friends, or read biographies and memoirs of couples who have navigated their lives together with love and commitment. These real-life examples can provide a grounded and relatable source of inspiration.

# Personal Anecdotes and Memories

**Celebrate Your Unique Journey**

Your own relationship is a goldmine of inspiration for your vows. Reflecting on personal anecdotes and memories can make your vows truly special and intimate. Here's how to incorporate them:

### Significant Moments

Think about the significant moments that have defined your relationship. This could be your first date, the moment you realized you were in love, or a memorable trip you took together. Including these moments in your vows can highlight the journey you've shared and the milestones you've reached together.

### Everyday Love

Sometimes, the beauty of a relationship lies in the small, everyday moments. Consider the little things your partner does that make you feel loved and appreciated. These could be gestures like making your morning coffee, a comforting hug after a tough day, or the way they make you laugh. Highlighting these everyday acts of love can add a personal and relatable touch to your vows.

### Overcoming Challenges

Reflect on the challenges you've faced together and how they have strengthened your bond. Whether it's supporting each other through difficult times, navigating long-distance, or overcoming personal obstacles, acknowledging these moments can show the resilience and depth of your love.

## Shared Dreams and Aspirations

Talk about your shared dreams and aspirations for the future. This not only reflects your commitment to a shared life but also emphasizes the hopes and plans you have together. Whether it's starting a family, traveling the world, or pursuing mutual passions, including these dreams can make your vows forward-looking and hopeful.

---

Finding inspiration for your wedding vows can come from a variety of sources, including books, movies, poetry, and real-life stories. However, the most meaningful inspiration often comes from your own relationship. By reflecting on personal anecdotes and memories, you can craft vows that are authentic and uniquely yours. Remember, your vows are a celebration of your journey together and a promise for the future, so let your love story shine through in every word.

# Writing Tools



Writing your wedding vows is a deeply personal and meaningful process that benefits from the right tools and materials. Having the proper resources can help you stay organized, capture your thoughts, and refine your vows into a polished final product. Here are some essential tools to consider:

Notebooks

A good notebook can be your best companion when writing your vows. Choose one that feels comfortable to write in and that you can easily carry with you. Here are some options:

- **Moleskine Notebooks:**
    - Known for their durability and quality paper, Moleskine notebooks are a classic choice.
- **Bullet Journals:**
    - If you prefer a more structured approach, bullet journals allow you to organize your thoughts with grids and customizable layouts.
- **Leather-Bound Journals:**
    - These provide a touch of elegance and can be a keepsake to look back on in the years to come.

Apps

For those who prefer digital tools, several apps can help you jot down ideas, organize your thoughts, and write your vows:

- **Evernote:**
    - This app is excellent for collecting ideas, notes, and references in one place. You can access it from multiple devices, making it easy to jot down thoughts on the go.
- **Google Keep:**
    - A simple and user-friendly app for taking quick notes, setting reminders, and organizing your ideas.
- **Scrivener:**
    - While its more advanced, Scrivener is fantastic for organizing complex writing projects and offers robust tools for structuring your vows.
- **Microsoft OneNote:**
    - This app is great for detailed note-taking and organizing your thoughts into different sections or categories.

In addition to notebooks and apps, other tools can aid in the writing process:

- **Voice Recorders:**
  - Sometimes, speaking your thoughts out loud can help clarify your ideas. Use a voice recorder or your smartphone to capture spontaneous thoughts and refine them later.
- **Index Cards:**
  - If you like to brainstorm in a non-linear fashion, index cards can be useful. You can write down individual ideas, quotes, or memories and then arrange them to find the best structure for your vows.
- **Writing Guides and Templates:**
  - Many books and online resources offer guides and templates for writing wedding vows. These can provide a helpful framework if you're unsure where to start.
- **Inspirational Quotes and Poems:**
  - Keep a collection of quotes, poems, and excerpts that resonate with you. These can serve as inspiration or even be included in your vows.

# Organizing Your Thoughts

### Mind Mapping

Mind mapping is a visual tool that can help you brainstorm and organize your ideas. Start with a central theme, such as "love" or "commitment," and branch out with related thoughts and memories. This method can help you see connections and structure your vows more clearly.

### Outline Your Vows

Create an outline to organize your thoughts and ensure a logical flow. A basic structure might include:

- **Introduction:**
  - A brief opening that sets the tone.
- **Body:**
  - Personal anecdotes, promises, and expressions of love.
- **Conclusion:**
  - A heartfelt closing statement.

### Set Goals and Deadlines

Establish a timeline for completing each stage of your vows, from brainstorming to final revisions. Setting goals and deadlines can help you stay on track and avoid last-minute stress.

Gathering the right materials and tools is an essential first step in writing your wedding vows. Whether you prefer traditional notebooks or digital apps, having the resources to capture and organize your thoughts can make the process smoother and more enjoyable. By using these tools, you can create vows that are heartfelt, meaningful, and a true reflection of your unique love story.

# ADDITIONAL TIPS...

**Set Aside Dedicated Time for Writing**

**Prioritize Time for Your Vows**

Writing your wedding vows is a task that deserves your full attention and dedication. Set aside specific times in your schedule solely for writing your vows. Here are some tips to help you make the most of this time:

**Create a Writing Schedule**

- **Consistent time Slots:**
  - Decide on regular times each week to focus on your vows. This could be an hour every Sunday morning or 30 minutes every evening after work. Consistency helps build momentum and keeps you on track.
- **Distraction-Free Environment:**
  - Find a quiet place where you won't be interrupted. Turn off your phone, close unnecessary tabs on your computer, and let those around you know that you need this time for yourself.
- **Set a Timer:**
  - If you find it hard to focus, use a timer to commit to short, intensive writing sessions. The Pomodoro Technique, which involves 25 minutes of focused work followed by a 5-minute break, can be particularly effective.

### Make It a Ritual

- **Inspire Creativity:**
  - Light a candle, play soft music, or have a cup of your favorite tea to create a calming atmosphere. These rituals can help signal to your brain that it's time to focus on writing.
- **Reflect and Relax:**
  - Start each writing session with a few minutes of reflection. Think about your partner, your relationship, and what you want to convey in your vows. This reflection can help center your thoughts and inspire your writing.

### Take Notes When Inspiration Strikes

### Capture Your Ideas

Inspiration can strike at any moment, and it's important to capture those thoughts immediately. Here are ways to ensure you don't lose those sparks of inspiration:

### Keep a Notebook Handy

- **Portable Notebook:**
  - Carry a small notebook with you at all times. Whether you're commuting, out for a walk, or lying in bed, having a notebook nearby allows you to jot down ideas as they come to you.

- **Dedicated Sections:**
  - Use different sections or pages for various themes, such as memories, promises, and future plans. This organization makes it easier to compile your thoughts later.

### Use Digital Tools

- **Note-Taking Apps:**
  - Utilize apps like Evernote, Google Keep, or the notes app on your phone to quickly record your thoughts. These apps are particularly useful because you can sync your notes across multiple devices.
- **Voice Memos:**
  - If you're driving or in a situation where writing isn't practical, use the voice memo feature on your phone to record your ideas verbally. Transcribe these notes later during your dedicated writing time.

## Discuss Your Thoughts with Your Partner

### Open Communication

While your vows are personal, discussing your thoughts and ideas with your partner can enhance the process. Here's how to approach these conversations:

### Set Aside Time to Talk

- **Schedule Discussions:**
  - Just as you schedule time for writing, set aside time to talk about your vows with your partner. These discussions can help you align your thoughts and ensure your vows complement each other.
- **Relaxed Setting:**
  - Choose a relaxed and comfortable setting for these talks, such as over a meal or during a walk. This can make the conversation feel more natural and less pressured.

### Share and Collaborate

- **Exchange Ideas:**
  - Share the themes, anecdotes, and promises you're considering for your vows. This exchange can spark new ideas and help you see different perspectives.
- **Feedback and Support:**
  - Offer constructive feedback and support to each other. This can help you refine your vows and ensure they are heartfelt and meaningful.
- **Respect Individuality:**
  - While collaboration is important, respect each other's individuality. Your vows should reflect your personal voice and feelings, even as they complement your partner's.

---

Writing your wedding vows is a deeply personal and important task that benefits from careful planning and thoughtful reflection. By setting aside dedicated time for writing, capturing inspiration when it strikes, and discussing your thoughts with your partner, you can create vows that truly reflect your love and commitment. These additional tips can help ensure that your vows are not only meaningful and sincere but also a true representation of your unique relationship.

# Reflecting on Your Relationship

**Your Journey Together**



## CHAPTER 03

**Key Moments and Milestones in Your Relationship**

Reflecting on the key moments and milestones in your relationship can help you write wedding vows that are deeply personal and meaningful. These moments form the foundation of your shared history and illustrate the growth and evolution of your love. Here's how to identify and incorporate them into your vows:

**First Meeting**

- **How You Met:**
  - Whether it was a chance encounter, a blind date, or an online meeting, recount the story of how you first met. This moment is the beginning of your journey and sets the stage for everything that followed.
- **First Impressions:**
  - Share your initial thoughts and feelings about your partner. Reflecting on these early impressions can be a charming and heartfelt addition to your vows.

- **Significance:**
  - Explain why this date stands out in your memory and how it made you feel more connected to your partner.

**First Meeting**

- **Details of the Date:**
  - Describe your first date, including where you went and what you did. Highlight any memorable moments or feelings you experienced.

## Falling in Love

- **Defining Moment:**
  - Think about the moment you realized you were in love with your partner. This can be a specific event or a gradual realization.
- **Emotional Impact:**
  - Describe the emotions you felt and how this realization changed your relationship.

## Key Milestones

- **Significant Events:**
  - Highlight major milestones in your relationship, such as moving in together, getting engaged, or other important events. These milestones mark your growth as a couple and your deepening commitment to each other.
- **Shared Achievements:**
  - Celebrate any accomplishments you've achieved together, whether it's graduating, buying a home, or achieving a mutual goal. These achievements show how you support and inspire each other.

## Everyday Moments

- **Daily Life:**
  - Sometimes the small, everyday moments are the most significant. Reflect on the routines, habits, and little gestures that define your daily life together.
- **Acts of Love:**
  - Mention the simple acts of love and kindness that make your relationship special, such as cooking dinner together, sharing a favorite hobby, or comforting each other after a long day.

# Challenges You've Overcome

Facing Adversity Together

Every relationship faces challenges, and overcoming them together can strengthen your bond and deepen your love. Reflecting on these challenges in your vows can show your resilience and commitment. Here's how to incorporate them:

Identifying Challenges

- **Personal Struggles:**
    - Think about any personal challenges each of you has faced, such as health issues, career setbacks, or personal growth struggles. Reflect on how your partner supported you during these times.
- **Relationship Challenges:**
    - Consider the challenges you've faced as a couple, such as long-distance, financial difficulties, or disagreements. Acknowledge how you worked through these challenges together.

Support and Strength

- **Mutual Support:**
    - Highlight the ways in which you supported each other during tough times. This could include providing emotional support, practical help, or simply being there for each other.
- **Growth and Resilience:**
    - Reflect on how these challenges helped you grow individually and as a couple. Discuss the lessons you've learned and how they've strengthened your relationship.

Commitment and Dedication

- **Reaffirming Commitment:**
    - Use these reflections to reaffirm your commitment to supporting each other through future challenges. Your vows can include promises to stand by each other, no matter what obstacles you face.
- **Celebrating Resilience:**
    - Celebrate the resilience and strength of your relationship. Acknowledge that overcoming challenges together has made your bond stronger and more enduring.

# Personal Growth



**Personal Growth and Development as a Couple**

Reflecting on how you and your partner have grown individually and as a couple can add depth and sincerity to your wedding vows. These reflections show the dynamic nature of your relationship and highlight the positive changes you've experienced together.


Individual Growth

- **Self-Discovery:**
    - Think about the ways in which your partner has encouraged you to discover new aspects of yourself. This might include pursuing new hobbies, developing new skills, or gaining new perspectives on life.
- **Overcoming Personal Challenges:**
    - Reflect on personal obstacles you've overcome with the support of your partner. Discuss how these experiences have made you stronger and more resilient.
- **Achievements:**
    - Highlight personal achievements that your partner has helped you accomplish. This could be in your career, education, or personal life.


Couple's Growth

- **Communication Skills:**
    - Consider how your communication has improved over time. Reflect on the ways you've learned to express your thoughts and feelings more openly and effectively.
- **Conflict Resolution:**
    - Acknowledge how you've grown in resolving conflicts. Discuss the strategies you've developed to navigate disagreements and maintain harmony in your relationship.
- **Shared Goals:**
    - Talk about how you've aligned your goals and aspirations as a couple. Reflect on the ways you've worked together to achieve mutual objectives, whether they're related to your personal lives, careers, or shared interests.

## Support and Encouragement

- **Emotional Support:**
  - Discuss how your partner has been there for you during difficult times, providing the emotional support you needed to overcome challenges.
- **Encouragement:**
  - Highlight the ways your partner has encouraged you to pursue your dreams and aspirations. Reflect on specific instances where their encouragement made a significant difference in your life.

## Learning and Growing Together

- **Learning from Each Other:**
  - Reflect on the valuable lessons you've learned from each other. This could include new ways of thinking, different perspectives on life, or practical skills.
- **Shared Experiences:**
  - Discuss the experiences you've shared that have contributed to your mutual growth. This could be travel, new activities, or simply spending time together in meaningful ways.

## Building a Stronger Bond

- **Trust and Intimacy:**
  - Talk about how your trust and intimacy have deepened over time. Reflect on the moments that have brought you closer and strengthened your bond.
- **Commitment to Each Other:**
  - Reaffirm your commitment to continue supporting each other's growth. Promise to always be there for each other, to encourage and uplift each other, and to face the future together as a team.

Reflecting on personal growth and mutual influence in your relationship adds a profound and meaningful dimension to your wedding vows. By acknowledging how you've changed individually and as a couple, and recognizing the support and encouragement you've provided each other, you create vows that are deeply personal and reflective of your unique journey together. This not only celebrates your past but also sets a strong foundation for your future, emphasizing the ongoing growth and development you will experience together.

# Shared Values



## Identifying What Binds You Together

Shared values are the cornerstone of a strong and enduring relationship. They form the foundation of your bond, guiding your decisions, actions, and interactions with each other. Reflecting on these core beliefs and values can help you articulate the principles that are most important to you as a couple. Here's how to identify and express them in your vows:

### Shared Values and Beliefs

- **Love and Respect:**
  - Highlight the importance of love and mutual respect in your relationship. Discuss how these values guide your actions and interactions with each other.
- **Honesty and Trust:**
  - Reflect on the significance of honesty and trust, and how these principles have strengthened your bond.
- **Kindness and Compassion:**
  - Consider the role of kindness and compassion in your relationship. Describe how you show care and understanding towards each other and others.
- **Family and Friendship:**
  - Discuss your shared commitment to family and friendship, and how these relationships enrich your lives.
- **Adventure and Growth:**
  - If adventure and personal growth are important to you, talk about your shared desire to explore new experiences and support each other's development.
- **Faith and Spirituality:**
  - If faith or spirituality plays a role in your lives, reflect on how these beliefs have shaped your relationship and guided your journey together.

- **Personal and Mutual Growth:**
  - Emphasize your commitment to supporting each other's personal growth and development. Promise to encourage and uplift each other as you pursue your individual and shared goals.
- **Learning Together:**
  - Pledge to continue learning and growing together, embracing new experiences and challenges as a team.

## Building a Life Together

- **Creating a Home:**
  - Reflect on your vision for creating a loving and supportive home. Discuss how your values will influence the environment you create for each other and any future family.
- **Making Decisions:**
  - Promise to base your decisions on your shared values, ensuring that your choices reflect your commitment to each other and your principles.

- **Resilience and Support**
    - Acknowledge that challenges will arise and pledge to face them together, drawing strength from your shared values. Promise to support each other through difficult times with love, respect, and understanding.
- **Adaptability:**
    - Highlight the importance of adaptability and flexibility, and how your values will help you navigate changes and uncertainties in life.

Creating Traditions

- **Shared Rituals:**
    - Discuss the traditions and rituals you want to create together, from daily habits to annual celebrations. Reflect on how these traditions will be rooted in your shared values.
- **Celebrating Milestones:**
    - Pledge to celebrate each milestone in your life together, honoring your journey and the principles that guide you.

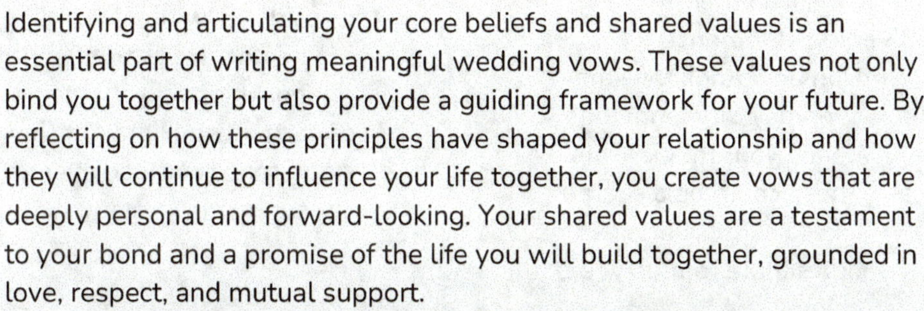

Identifying and articulating your core beliefs and shared values is an essential part of writing meaningful wedding vows. These values not only bind you together but also provide a guiding framework for your future. By reflecting on how these principles have shaped your relationship and how they will continue to influence your life together, you create vows that are deeply personal and forward-looking. Your shared values are a testament to your bond and a promise of the life you will build together, grounded in love, respect, and mutual support.

# ADDITIONAL TIPS...

**Make a List of Memorable Moments
Reflect on Your Journey**

Taking the time to list memorable moments from your relationship can provide a rich source of inspiration for your wedding vows. These moments encapsulate the essence of your journey together and highlight the unique bond you share. Here's how to approach this:

**Identify Key Moments**

- **Firsts:**
  - Recall your first meeting, first date, first "I love you," and other significant firsts. These moments are often filled with strong emotions and pivotal realizations.
- **Special Occasions:**
  - Think about holidays, birthdays, anniversaries, and other celebrations you've shared. These occasions often highlight your connection and love for each other.
- **Everyday Moments:**
  - Don't overlook the small, everyday moments that define your relationship. These could be a shared joke, a comforting gesture, or a simple routine you both enjoy.

**Describe the Emotions**

- **Feelings and Thoughts:**
  - Reflect on how you felt during these memorable moments. Describe the emotions you experienced and what these moments meant to you.
- **Impact:**
  - Consider how these moments have shaped your relationship and your view of each other. Highlight the significance of these events in your journey together.

- **Storytelling:**
  - Use these memorable moments to tell a story in your vows. Paint a vivid picture that transports your partner and your guests back to those special times.
- **Personal Touch:**
  - By including specific memories, you add a personal touch to your vows, making them unique and deeply meaningful.

## Highlight the Qualities You Admire in Your Partner

### Celebrate Your Partner

Expressing the qualities you admire in your partner is a beautiful way to show your love and appreciation. These qualities form the foundation of your admiration and respect for each other. Here's how to highlight them in your vows:

### List Their Best Traits

- **Character Traits:**
  - Think about the character traits you admire most in your partner, such as kindness, generosity, patience, or a sense of humor.
- **Talents and Skills:**
  - Reflect on their talents and skills, whether it's their ability to solve problems, their creativity, or their professional achievements.
- **Actions and Behaviors:**
  - Consider the actions and behaviors that make you love and respect them, like how they treat others, their work ethic, or their commitment to your relationship.

### Provide Examples

- **Specific Instances:**
  - Give specific examples of when your partner displayed these admirable qualities. These examples can make your admiration more tangible and relatable.
- **Everyday Gestures:**
  - Highlight the everyday gestures that make you feel loved and appreciated. These small acts often have a big impact on your relationship.

- **Acknowledge Their Impact:**
  - Acknowledge how these qualities have positively influenced your life and your relationship. Express your gratitude for having such an incredible partner.
- **Pledge to Honor Them:**
  - Promise to honor and cherish these qualities in your partner, and to support them in continuing to grow and shine.



### Look to the Future

Considering your shared dreams and goals can help you write vows that are not only reflective of your past and present but also forward-looking. These aspirations show your commitment to building a future together. Here's how to incorporate them into your vows:

### Identify Your Dreams

- **Long-Term Goals:**
  - Discuss your long-term goals as a couple, such as starting a family, traveling the world, buying a home, or pursuing certain careers.

- **Short-Term Aspirations:**
  - Reflect on your short-term aspirations, like planning a special trip, learning a new skill together, or achieving a milestone..

### Discuss Your Shared Vision

- **Future Plans:**
  - Talk about your plans for the future and how you envision your life together. This could include where you want to live, the kind of lifestyle you hope to have, and the experiences you want to share.
- **Personal Growth:**
  - Reflect on how you plan to grow individually and as a couple. Discuss your commitment to supporting each other's personal development and shared aspirations.

- **Promises for the Future:**
  - Make specific promises related to your shared dreams and goals. For example, you might vow to support each other's career ambitions, to explore new places together, or to build a loving home.
- **Shared Journey:**
  - Emphasize that your journey together is ongoing and that you are excited about the future you will create together. Express your commitment to facing whatever comes your way, united in your shared vision.

By making a list of memorable moments, highlighting the qualities you admire in your partner, and thinking about your shared dreams and goals, you can create wedding vows that are deeply personal, meaningful, and forward-looking. These additional tips can help ensure that your vows reflect the unique journey you've shared, the admiration and respect you have for each other, and the exciting future you are committed to building together.

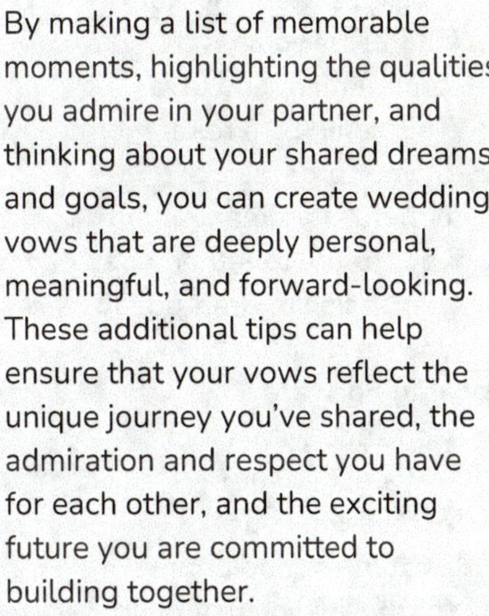

# Structuring Your Vows



Writing wedding vows can be a daunting task, but breaking them down into manageable components can help you craft something truly special. Understanding the anatomy of a vow and finding a balance between personal anecdotes and universal truths will ensure your vows are both meaningful and relatable.

## Components of a Vow

### Introduction

- **Opening Statement:**
    - Start with a heartfelt opening that captures the essence of your love. This could be a quote, a reflection on your relationship, or a simple but powerful statement of love.
- **Setting the Tone:**
    - Your introduction sets the tone for the rest of your vows. Decide whether you want it to be romantic, humorous, sincere, or a mix of these.

### Body

- **Personal Anecdotes:**
    - Share specific memories and experiences that highlight your relationship's journey. These stories make your vows unique and personal.
- **Promises and Commitments:**
    - Outline the promises you are making to your partner. These can range from the profound ("I promise to always support you") to the light-hearted ("I promise to never hog the TV remote").
- **Qualities You Admire:**
    - Mention the traits and qualities you love and admire in your partner. This shows appreciation and highlights what makes your partner special to you.

### Conclusion

- **Final Pledge:**
    - End with a powerful closing statement that reinforces your commitment and love. This could be a reiteration of your promises, a hopeful statement about your future together, or an expression of gratitude for your partner.
- **Looking Forward:**
    - Conclude with a look towards the future, expressing your excitement and optimism for the life you will build together.

Introduction, Body, and Conclusion

## Introduction

- **Capturing Attention:**
    - Begin with something that grabs attention. This could be a personal reflection, a meaningful quote, or a heartfelt statement.
- Example:
    - "From the moment I first saw you, I knew you were someone special."

## Body

- **Personal Stories:**
    - Incorporate anecdotes that illustrate the depth of your relationship. Choose moments that were significant to you both and explain why they matter.
- Example:
    - "I remember our first road trip together, getting lost and discovering that we both loved the same obscure band. It was in those moments of spontaneity and shared joy that I knew I wanted to spend my life with you."
- Promises:
    - Make your promises specific and heartfelt. They should reflect both your hopes and your realistic commitment to the relationship.
- Example:
    - "I promise to always be your biggest supporter and to cherish every moment we share, whether it's a grand adventure or a quiet evening at home."

## Conclusion

- **Final Thoughts:**
    - Summarize your feelings and reiterate your commitment. This is your chance to leave a lasting impression with your words.
- Example:
    - "As we stand here today, I look forward to a future filled with love, laughter, and countless memories. I am honored to become your partner for life."

## Balancing Personal Anecdotes with Universal Truths

### Personal Anecdotes

- **Specificity:**
  - Personal stories make your vows unique and memorable. They highlight your shared history and bring out the personality of your relationship.
- Example:
  - "I knew you were the one for me when you stayed up all night helping me finish my project, even though you had work the next morning."

### Universal Truths

- **Relatability:**
  - While personal stories are crucial, weaving in universal truths about love and commitment can make your vows resonate with your partner and your audience.
- Example:
  - "Love is about finding someone who brings out the best in you, who supports you through the highs and lows. With you, I've found all that and more."

### Finding the Balance

- **Integrating Both:**
  - Blend personal anecdotes with universal truths to create a vow that is both deeply personal and widely relatable.
- Example:
  - "From the day we met, I knew our connection was special. You've taught me that true love is patient and kind, and I vow to embody those qualities in our marriage."

Structuring your vows with a clear introduction, body, and conclusion will help you create a cohesive and meaningful expression of your love. Balancing personal anecdotes with universal truths ensures that your vows are both unique to your relationship and relatable to everyone who hears them. By breaking down the components and carefully crafting each section, you can write vows that truly capture the essence of your commitment and love.

# Length and Format

### Finding the Right Balance

When writing your wedding vows, it's important to strike a balance between being concise and being meaningful. Here's how to achieve that balance:

### Keeping it Concise but Meaningful

- **Set a Time Limit:**
  - Aim for your vows to be between one and two minutes long. This typically translates to around 150-250 words. This length is enough to express your feelings without losing the audience's attention.
- **Focus on Key Points:**
  - Identify the most important messages you want to convey. Focus on these points rather than trying to include every thought or memory.
- **Edit Ruthlessly:**
  - Write a draft and then trim it down. Remove any redundant or less impactful sentences to ensure every word adds value.
- **Practice Reading Aloud:**
  - Reading your vows aloud can help you gauge their length and emotional impact. Make adjustments to keep them concise and powerful.

### Deciding on a Tone and Style

The tone and style of your vows should reflect your personality and the nature of your relationship. Consider the following approaches:

### Romantic and Sincere

- **Language:**
  - Use heartfelt and loving language to express your deep feelings and commitment.
- **Example:**
  - "I promise to love you unconditionally, to support you through all of life's challenges, and to cherish every moment we share."

### Humorous and Light-hearted

- **Language:**
  - Incorporate humor and light-hearted anecdotes to reflect your playful side.
- **Example:**
  - "I promise to always let you have the last piece of pizza, even though I secretly want it."

### Traditional and Formal

- **Language:**
  - Use more formal and traditional language, drawing inspiration from classic vows.
- **Example:**
  - "I take you to be my lawfully wedded spouse, to have and to hold, in sickness and in health, for richer or poorer, as long as we both shall live."

### Personal and Unique

- **Language:**
  - Use a mix of personal anecdotes, inside jokes, and heartfelt promises that are unique to your relationship.
- **Example:**
  - "I promise to always cheer for your favorite team, even when they're losing, and to be your co-adventurer in all of life's journeys."

### Combining Tones

- **Balanced Approach:**
  - Combine elements of different tones to suit your personality and relationship. For instance, start with a humorous anecdote and end with a heartfelt promise.
- **Example:**
  - "I promise to never watch the next episode without you, and to always be your shoulder to lean on."

Finding the right balance in length and format for your wedding vows involves being concise yet meaningful, and choosing a tone and style that reflects your relationship. By setting a time limit, focusing on key points, and practicing your vows aloud, you can ensure they are impactful and memorable. Whether you choose a romantic, humorous, traditional, or personal style, or a combination of these, the most important thing is that your vows genuinely reflect your love and commitment to your partner.

# Flow and Coherence

## Creating a Narrative

Your wedding vows should tell a story—a narrative that reflects your journey together, your love, and your promises for the future. Here's how to create a narrative that flows smoothly and is both engaging and heartfelt.

### Beginning: Setting the Stage

- **Start with a Hook:**
  - Begin with a compelling statement, a memorable moment, or a quote that sets the tone for your vows. This will capture your audience's attention and provide a strong starting point.
    - Example:
      - "From the first moment I saw you, I knew my life was about to change forever."
- **Introduce Your Relationship:**
  - Briefly outline the key moments that brought you to this point. This helps set the context for your vows.
    - Example:
      - "We met in a crowded coffee shop, and over countless cups of coffee and late-night conversations, our friendship blossomed into a love I had never imagined."

- **Share Personal Anecdotes:**
  - Highlight significant moments in your relationship that have shaped your journey together. These stories make your vows personal and relatable.
    - Example:
      - "I'll never forget the time we got lost on our road trip and ended up discovering the most beautiful little town. It's in those unexpected moments that I fell even more in love with you."
- **Express Emotions and Insights:**
  - Talk about the emotions you've experienced and the insights you've gained from your relationship. This adds depth to your narrative.
    - Example:
      - "Through our ups and downs, I've learned the true meaning of unconditional love and unwavering support."
- **Make Promises:**
  - State the promises you are making to your partner. These should be specific, meaningful, and reflective of your journey together.
    - Example:
      - "I promise to always be your biggest supporter, to laugh with you in joy, and to comfort you in sorrow."

End: Looking Forward

- **Conclude with a Vision for the Future:**
  - End your vows with a forward-looking statement that reflects your hopes and dreams for your life together.
    - Example:
      - "As we stand here today, I look forward to a future filled with adventure, love, and endless possibilities with you by my side."
- **Reiterate Your Commitment:**
  - Reinforce your commitment and love for your partner. This leaves a lasting impression and provides a strong closing.
    - Example:
      - "No matter what the future holds, I am committed to loving you, growing with you, and building a beautiful life together."

# Ensuring a Smooth Transition Between Sections

## Use Transitional Phrases

- **Connecting Ideas:**
  - Use transitional phrases to smoothly connect different parts of your vows. This ensures your narrative flows seamlessly from one section to the next.
    - Example:
      - "From our first date to this moment, every day has been an adventure. Speaking of adventures, I remember when…"
- **Highlighting Changes:**
  - Indicate shifts in focus or topic with phrases that guide your audience through your story.
    - Example:
      - "While those memories are dear to me, I also cherish the everyday moments we share…"

## Maintain a Logical Order

- **Chronological Order:**
  - Organize your vows in a logical sequence, such as chronologically, to make it easy for your audience to follow your narrative.
    - Example:
      - "First, we built a foundation of friendship, then we shared countless adventures, and now we stand here ready to embark on a new journey together."
- **Thematic Order:**
  - Alternatively, you can organize your vows thematically, focusing on different aspects of your relationship, such as trust, support, and love.
    - Example:
      - "Your unwavering support, your endless kindness, and your boundless love have made me a better person…"

# Making Your Vows Engaging and Heartfelt

Be Genuine and Authentic

- **Speak from the Heart:**
  - Let your true feelings shine through. Authenticity resonates deeply and makes your vows more engaging.
    - Example:
      - "I love you more than words can express, and I am so grateful to have you as my partner in life."

Use Vivid Language

- **Paint a Picture:**
  - Use descriptive language to create vivid images and emotions. This helps your audience connect with your story.
    - Example:
      - "Your smile lights up my darkest days, and your laughter is the melody that fills my heart with joy."

Incorporate Humor and Light-hearted Moments

- **Balance Seriousness with Light-heartedness:**
  - Including humor can make your vows more relatable and enjoyable.
    - Example:
      - "I promise to always let you choose the movie, even if it's another cheesy rom-com."

Showcase Your Unique Relationship

- **Highlight What Makes Your Relationship Special:**
  - Focus on the unique aspects of your relationship that set it apart.
    - Example:
      - "No one else understands my love for late-night ice cream runs like you do, and I promise to always be your partner in crime for all our spontaneous adventures."

# ADDITIONAL TIPS...

Writing wedding vows can be both an exciting and daunting task. To help streamline the process and ensure your vows are heartfelt and polished, consider the following additional tips:

**Use Bullet Points to Organize Your Thoughts**

**Benefits of Bullet Points**

- **Clarity and Structure:**
  - Bullet points help you break down your ideas into clear, manageable sections.
- **Focus:**
  - They allow you to focus on individual aspects of your vows without feeling overwhelmed by the entire task.
- **Ease of Editing:**
  - Bullet points make it easier to rearrange and edit your thoughts before committing to a full draft.

**How to Use Bullet Points**

- **Brainstorming:**
  - List all the ideas, promises, and memories you want to include in your vows.

- **Example:**
  - First met at a coffee shop
  - Road trip to the beach
  - Promise to support each other's dreams
  - Love for late-night ice cream runs
- **Organizing:**
  - Group related ideas together to form the structure of your vows (introduction, body, conclusion).
    - **Example:**
      - Introduction:
        - First met at a coffee shop

- Body:
  - Road trip to the beach
  - love for late-night ice cream runs
  - Promise to support each other's dreams
- Conclusion:
  - Looking forward to a future filled with adventure

## Write Multiple Drafts to Refine Your Vows

### Importance of Multiple Drafts

- **Improvement:**
  - Each draft allows you to refine your language, improve the flow, and ensure clarity.
- **Focus:**
  - Rewriting helps you focus on the most important messages and remove any redundant or less impactful content.
- **Polish:**
  - Multiple drafts ensure that your final vows are polished and thoughtfully composed.

### How to Approach Drafting

- **First Draft:**
  - Write freely without worrying about length or perfection. Focus on getting all your thoughts and feelings down on paper.
- **Second Draft:**
  - Edit for clarity and structure. Organize your vows into a cohesive narrative with a clear beginning, middle, and end.
- **Subsequent Drafts:**
  - Refine your language, ensure smooth transitions, and balance personal anecdotes with universal truths. Aim for conciseness while retaining meaningful content.
- **Final Draft:**
  - Polish your vows for final presentation. Check for grammar, spelling, and overall coherence.

## Practice Reading Your Vows Aloud to Gauge Length and Flow

### Benefits of Practicing Aloud

- **Length:**
  - Reading aloud helps you gauge the actual length of your vows and ensure they fit within the desired time frame.
- **Flow:**
  - It helps you identify any awkward phrasing or areas where the flow may be disrupted.
- **Comfort:**
  - Practicing aloud increases your comfort and confidence in delivering your vows on the big day.

### How to Practice

- **Solo Practice:**
  - Start by reading your vows aloud to yourself. Make notes of any sections that feel too long, awkward, or unclear.
- **Feedback:**
  - Practice in front of a trusted friend or family member and ask for constructive feedback. This can provide new insights and suggestions for improvement.
- **Final Rehearsal:**
  - As the wedding day approaches, practice reading your vows aloud in a similar setting to the ceremony. This helps you get comfortable with the delivery and timing.

Using bullet points to organize your thoughts, writing multiple drafts to refine your vows, and practicing reading your vows aloud are effective strategies to ensure your wedding vows are well-structured, meaningful, and engaging. These additional tips can help you create vows that truly reflect your love and commitment, making your wedding ceremony even more memorable and heartfelt.

# Writing with Emotion and Authenticity

Your wedding vows are an opportunity to express your deepest feelings and promises to your partner. To make them truly special, it's essential to write with emotion and authenticity. This chapter will guide you in finding your voice and ensuring your vows are heartfelt and genuine.

## Finding Your Voice

### Be Yourself

- **Speak Naturally:**
  - Write your vows as if you're speaking directly to your partner. Use your natural tone and vocabulary to ensure your vows sound like you.
    - Example:
      - Instead of saying "I vow to cherish you eternally," you might say, "I promise to always have your back."
- **Show Your Personality:**
  - Infuse your personality into your vows. If you're naturally humorous, don't be afraid to include a light-hearted joke or playful promise. If you're more serious, focus on heartfelt and sincere expressions.
    - Example:
      - "I promise to be your partner in crime and your biggest fan, no matter what adventures life throws our way."

### Authenticity Over Perfection

- **Focus on Sincerity:**
  - It's more important that your vows are sincere and genuine than perfectly worded. Authenticity resonates more deeply than scripted perfection.
    - Example:
      - "I may not always have the right words, but my love for you is beyond words. I promise to show you every day how much you mean to me."
- **Embrace Imperfections:**
  - Don't stress about getting every word right. It's okay if your vows aren't perfectly polished. What matters most is that they come from the heart.
    - Example:
      - "I might stumble over my words today, but I'll never stumble in my love for you."

- **Reflect Your Relationship:**
  - Think about the nature of your relationship and let that guide your writing. If your relationship is full of adventure, your vows might reflect that spirit. If it's built on quiet, steady love, your vows might be more contemplative.
    - Example:
      - "From our spontaneous road trips to our cozy nights in, I promise to cherish every moment we share."
- **Avoid Clichés:**
  - While it's okay to be inspired by traditional vows, make sure your words are specific to your relationship. Avoid overused phrases and focus on what makes your bond unique.
    - Example:
      - Instead of "I'll love you forever," try "I promise to love you through every sunrise and sunset, through every challenge and triumph."

- **Use Personal Anecdotes:**
  - Sharing personal stories and experiences makes your vows unique and memorable. These anecdotes should reflect significant moments in your relationship and highlight why your partner is so special to you.
    - Example:
      - "I knew I loved you when you stayed up all night helping me finish my project, even though you had work the next day. Your selflessness and support mean everything to me."

Writing with emotion and authenticity is key to crafting wedding vows that are heartfelt and memorable. By finding your voice, being yourself, prioritizing authenticity over perfection, and writing in a way that feels true to you, you'll create vows that genuinely reflect your love and commitment. These principles will help ensure your vows are a beautiful and sincere expression of your relationship, making your wedding day even more special.

# Evoking Emotion and Expressing Deep Feelings

Writing wedding vows that resonate emotionally requires using language that conveys your deepest feelings while striking a balance between humor, sincerity, and passion. Here's how to achieve that:

## Using Language that Conveys Your Emotions

### Choosing the Right Words

- **Be Descriptive:**
  - Use vivid language that paints a picture of your emotions. Describe how your partner makes you feel and why they are special to you.
    - Example:
      - "Your laughter fills my days with joy, and your touch brings warmth to even the coldest nights."
- **Express Gratitude:**
  - Show appreciation for your partner and the impact they've had on your life. Acknowledge what they bring to the relationship.
    - Example:
      - "I am grateful for your unwavering support and the way you always believe in me, even when I doubt myself."

- **Highlight Shared Moments:**
  - Recall specific memories or shared experiences that have shaped your relationship. This adds depth and personalizes your vows.
    - Example:
      - "From our first date to this day, every moment with you has been a treasure. I cherish the memories we've created and look forward to many more."

Balancing Humor, Sincerity, and Passion

## Humor

- **Be Descriptive:**
  - Inject humor with anecdotes or promises that reflect your relationship's playful side. This shows your ability to laugh together.
    - **Example:**
      - "I promise to always let you have the last slice of pizza, even though I secretly want it."

## Sincerity

- **Heartfelt Promises:**
  - Make sincere promises that reflect your commitment and devotion to your partner. Speak from the heart about your hopes and dreams together.
    - **Example:**
      - "I promise to stand by your side, through every triumph and challenge, and to love you with all my heart for all our days."

## Passion

- **Expressing Love:**
  - Use passionate language to express the depth of your love and desire for a future together. Let your partner know how deeply you care.
    - **Example:**
      - "You are my soulmate, my best friend, and my greatest adventure. I cannot wait to build our life together, hand in hand."

When writing your wedding vows, it's important to steer clear of clichés and instead focus on creating a personal and meaningful expression of your love and commitment. Here's how to avoid clichés and personalize traditional elements:

## Steering Clear of Overused Phrases

### Identifying Clichés:

- **Common Phrases to Avoid:**
  - Examples include "You complete me," "You are my everything," or "I promise to love you forever."
- Why Avoid Them:
  - Clichés can feel insincere and fail to capture the uniqueness of your relationship. They may also lack the personal touch that makes vows meaningful.

## Personalizing Traditional Elements

- **Modify Traditional Vows:**
  - Take inspiration from traditional vows but put your own spin on them. Personalize the language to reflect your specific relationship and shared experiences.
    - Example:
      - Instead of saying, "To have and to hold," you might say, "To cherish and support, through all of life's adventures."

- **Incorporate Shared Moments:**
  - Include anecdotes or memories that are unique to your relationship. This adds depth and authenticity to your vows.
    - Example:
      - "I promise to always remember our spontaneous road trips and the laughter we shared along the way."

**Focus on Specifics:**

- **Use Specific Details:**
  - Describe qualities and actions that are unique to your partner and your relationship. This demonstrates your deep knowledge and appreciation.
    - **Example:**
      - "I love the way you make coffee every morning just the way I like it, with an extra sprinkle of cinnamon, because you know it's my favorite."
- **Share Inside Jokes or Nicknames:**
  - Incorporate elements that are meaningful and special to just the two of you. This adds intimacy and humor to your vows.
    - **Example:**
      - "I promise to always laugh at your cheesy jokes and continue our tradition of 'Pizza Fridays,' even when it's Tuesday."

## Crafting a Personal Narrative

**Tell Your Story:**

- **Highlight Milestones:**
  - Reflect on key moments in your relationship journey. Share how these moments have shaped your love and commitment.
    - **Example:**
      - "From our first date at that little café to the day we adopted our first pet, each moment with you has deepened my love."
- **Express Future Hopes:**
  - Talk about your dreams and aspirations as a couple. Share what excites you about the future and how you envision your life together.
    - **Example:**
      - "I look forward to exploring new places with you, building a home filled with laughter and love, and growing old together."

## Review and Refine:

- **Edit with Care:**
    - Read through your vows and remove any clichés or generic phrases. Replace them with personal sentiments and specific details.
- **Seek Feedback:**
    - Share your vows with close friends or family members to ensure they capture your unique bond and resonate authentically.

By avoiding clichés and infusing your vows with personal details and unique elements, you can create a heartfelt and memorable expression of your love and commitment. Personalizing traditional elements and focusing on specifics that are meaningful to your relationship will ensure your vows are authentic and deeply resonant on your wedding day. These tips will help you craft vows that are as special and unique as your love for each other.

# ADDITIONAL TIPS...

Writing wedding vows is a deeply personal and emotional task. To ensure your vows are authentic and memorable, consider these additional tips:

**Write as You Speak; Let Your Natural Voice Shine**

- **Speak from the Heart:**
  - Write your vows in a way that reflects how you naturally communicate with your partner. Use your everyday language and expressions to convey your feelings.
    - **Example:**
      - Instead of using formal language, say, "I promise to always be there for you, no matter what life throws our way."

- **Be Genuine:**
  - Authenticity is key. Your vows should sound like you and reflect your personality and relationship. Avoid using overly formal or stiff language that doesn't resonate with who you are.

- **Example:**
  - "I can't wait to spend forever with you" might be more genuine than "I eagerly anticipate a lifelong journey together."

Don't Shy Away from Showing Vulnerability

- **Embrace Emotional Depth:**
  - It's okay to express vulnerability and raw emotions in your vows. Share your fears, hopes, and dreams with your partner.
    - Example:
      - "I promise to always be honest with you, even when it's hard, because you deserve nothing less than my full truth."
- **Share Personal Insights:**
  - Reflect on moments of growth or challenges you've faced together. Showing vulnerability fosters intimacy and strengthens your bond.
    - Example:
      - "Through our highs and lows, I've learned that love is not just a feeling but a choice I make every day to be by your side."

Focus on What Makes Your Relationship Unique

- **Highlight Your Story:**
  - Celebrate the moments, traditions, and inside jokes that define your relationship. These personal touches make your vows meaningful and memorable.
    - Example:
      - "I promise to always support your obsession with hiking, even if I prefer cozy evenings at home. Together, we find the perfect balance."
- **Showcase Shared Values:**
  - Express how your shared values and beliefs shape your commitment to each other. This strengthens the foundation of your vows..
    - Example:
      - "Our shared love for family and our commitment to always prioritize each other's happiness make me confident that we can conquer anything together."

By writing in your natural voice, embracing vulnerability, and focusing on the unique aspects of your relationship, you can create wedding vows that are deeply personal and meaningful. These tips will help you express your love and commitment authentically, making your wedding ceremony a cherished moment for both you and your partner.

# Practical Considerations

Wedding vows are not only a personal expression of love but also an opportunity to honor traditions and incorporate meaningful elements into your ceremony. This chapter explores how to balance and personalize traditions to create vows that reflect your unique relationship.

## Balancing Traditions

### Understanding the Importance of Traditions

- **Meaning and Symbolism:**
  - Traditions often carry deep cultural or familial significance. They can add richness and depth to your wedding ceremony.
    - Example:
      - Incorporating a unity candle ceremony to symbolize the merging of two families into one.
- **Respecting Family Wishes:**
  - Discuss with your families if there are specific traditions they hold dear. Finding a compromise that respects both your wishes and theirs can be a meaningful gesture.
    - Example:
      - Including a prayer or blessing from your cultural or religious background.

## Honoring Traditions

### Incorporating Traditional Elements

- **Research and Understand:**
  - Take time to research the traditions you wish to include. Understand their origins and meanings to ensure they align with your values.
    - Example:
      - Including a traditional dance from your cultural heritage during the reception.
- **Personalizing Traditions:**
  - Put your own twist on traditional elements to make them meaningful and reflective of your relationship.
    - Example:
      - Writing your own vows within the framework of a traditional ceremony.

## CHAPTER 06

## Adding Personal Touches

- **Reflect Your Relationship:**
  - Incorporate elements that resonate with your journey as a couple. This could be anything from favorite songs to shared hobbies.
    - Example:
      - Creating a custom ritual that symbolizes a shared passion, like planting a tree together during the ceremony.
- **Writing Personal Vows:**
  - Even within a traditional ceremony, writing personal vows allows you to express your unique promises and commitments to each other.
    - Example:
      - Combining traditional vows with personalized promises that reflect your values and aspirations as a couple.

## Final Tips

- **Communication is Key:**
  - Discuss your ideas for incorporating traditions with your partner and families early in the planning process. This ensures everyone feels included and respected.
- **Stay True to Yourselves:**
  - Don't feel pressured to include traditions that don't resonate with you. Choose elements that feel meaningful and authentic to your relationship.

Balancing and personalizing traditions in your wedding vows allows you to honor the past while celebrating your unique love story. Whether you choose to incorporate cultural, religious, or family traditions, or create new ones of your own, the key is to make your vows a reflection of who you are as individuals and as a couple. By honoring traditions in a way that feels authentic, you create a meaningful and memorable wedding ceremony that sets the tone for your future together.

# Understanding Religious and Cultural Diversity

## Research and Dialogue

- **Educate Yourself:**
  - Take the time to research and understand the religious and cultural backgrounds of both families. This includes traditions, values, and significant rituals.
    - Example:
      - Study the meanings behind specific prayers, ceremonies, or customs from each tradition.
- **Open Communication:**
  - Engage in open and respectful discussions with your partner and families. Seek to understand their perspectives and preferences regarding the incorporation of religious or cultural elements.
    - Example:
      - Discussing with both families how to best represent their beliefs in the ceremony.

## Finding Common Ground

### Identifying Shared Values

- **Focus on Universal Principles:**
  - Highlight values that are universally respected across different religions and cultures. Incorporate these into your vows to resonate with both families.
    - Example:
      - Promising love, respect, commitment, and support in ways that align with shared human values.
- **Inclusive Language:**
  - Use language in your vows that is inclusive and respectful of diverse beliefs. Avoid exclusivist or sectarian language that may alienate or offend anyone present.
    - Example:
      - Instead of specific religious references, use broader terms like "spiritual journey" or "shared faith in love."

## Balancing Traditions

- **Personalize Your Vows:**
  - Write vows that reflect your unique relationship while respecting the beliefs and traditions of both families. Blend personal promises with cultural or religious elements where appropriate.
    - **Example:**
      - Incorporating blessings or prayers from each tradition that hold special meaning for your families.
- **Seek Guidance:**
  - Consider consulting with religious or cultural leaders who can provide guidance on respectful ways to incorporate traditions into your vows.
    - **Example:**
      - Asking a religious officiant or cultural advisor for advice on weaving traditions into your ceremony.

## Final Considerations

- **Consensus Building:**
  - Aim to reach consensus among all parties involved regarding the inclusion of religious or cultural elements. Ensure that everyone feels valued and respected.
- **Flexibility:**
  - Be open to adjustments and compromises that accommodate different beliefs and preferences. Flexibility can foster harmony and inclusivity in your wedding ceremony.

Respecting religious and cultural sensitivities in your wedding vows is essential for creating a ceremony that honors both families and celebrates your love authentically. By understanding, communicating, and incorporating traditions thoughtfully, you can ensure that your vows reflect the diversity and richness of your backgrounds, uniting both families in joyous celebration on your special day. These considerations will help you craft vows that are meaningful, respectful, and inclusive, setting a tone of harmony and love for your future together.

# Deciding Whether to Write Vows Separately or Together

## Understanding Your Preferences

- **Discuss Preferences:**
  - Begin by discussing with your partner how you both envision your vows. Decide whether you want to write them separately or collaborate on them.
    - Example:
      - "Would you prefer we write our vows separately and surprise each other, or would you like to work on them together to ensure they reflect both of our voices?"
- **Consider Individual Styles:**
  - Take into account your individual writing styles and preferences. Some couples may prefer the surprise of hearing each other's vows for the first time during the ceremony.
    - Example:
      - "I think it would be meaningful for us to keep our vows a secret until the wedding day."

## Sharing Ideas Without Giving Everything Away

### Maintaining Surprise

- **Setting Boundaries:**
  - Agree on boundaries for sharing ideas. Share themes, sentiments, or key elements of your vows without revealing the entire content.
    - Example:
      - "Let's discuss the emotions we want to convey and any special promises we have in mind, but keep the specific words a surprise."
- **Respecting Privacy:**
  - Respect each other's desire for personal expression and the element of surprise. Avoid reading each other's complete vows until the wedding day to preserve the emotional impact.
    - Example:
      - "I trust that your vows will be beautiful and heartfelt, and I'm excited to hear them during our ceremony."

# Collaboration Benefits

- **Strengthening Your Bond:**
  - Working together on your vows can deepen your connection and understanding of each other's values and aspirations.
- **Ensuring Alignment:**
  - Collaborating allows you to ensure your vows reflect both of your personalities and the shared journey you're embarking on together.

# Final Tips

- **Enjoy the Process:**
  - Writing your vows together can be a meaningful and enjoyable experience. Embrace the opportunity to express your love and commitment in a way that feels authentic to both of you.
- **Celebrate Your Unique Relationship:**
  - Whether you write separately or together, remember that your vows are a celebration of your unique relationship and the love you share.

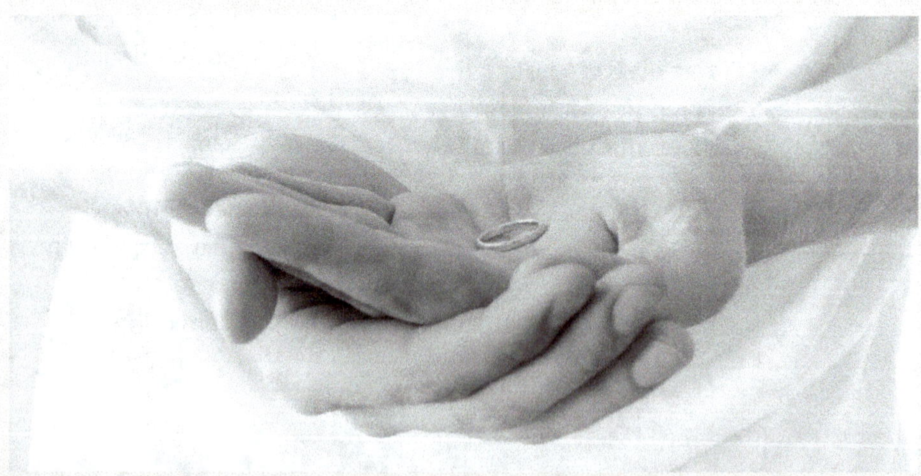

# ADDITIONAL TIPS...

Writing wedding vows is an emotional and personal experience. Here are some additional tips to help you navigate the process smoothly:

### Managing Emotions

- **Prepare a Backup Plan:**
  - It's natural to feel emotional while reading your vows. Have a plan in place if you become overwhelmed, such as taking a deep breath or pausing briefly.
    - Example:
      - "If I get emotional, I'll take a moment to compose myself before continuing."
- **Practice Self-Care:**
  - Prioritize self-care in the days leading up to your wedding. This can help manage emotions and ensure you feel grounded during the ceremony.

### Seeking Feedback

- **Use a Sounding Board:**
  - Share your vows with a trusted friend or family member for feedback. They can offer perspective and help ensure your vows are clear and impactful.
    - Example:
      - "Could you listen to my vows and provide feedback on how they sound?"
- **Maintain Surprise:**
  - If sharing your vows with someone, ensure they understand the importance of keeping them confidential until the ceremony.

- **Review Each Other's Vows:**
  - If writing separately, review each other's vows to ensure they complement one another in tone and content.
    - Example:
      - "Let's read each other's vows beforehand to ensure they flow well together."
- **Coordinate Themes:**
  - Discuss overarching themes or promises to avoid redundancy or conflicting messages in your vows.
    - Example:
      - "Let's ensure our vows complement each other by focusing on different aspects of our relationship."

By preparing for emotional moments, seeking feedback from trusted individuals, and ensuring cohesion between your vows, you can create a memorable and heartfelt expression of your love and commitment. These tips will help you navigate the process of writing and delivering your vows with confidence and authenticity on your wedding day.

# Revising and Polishing Your Vows

Once you have written the first draft of your wedding vows, the next crucial step is revising and polishing them. This chapter guides you through the revision process, offering techniques for refining your vows and emphasizing the importance of multiple drafts.



## CHAPTER 07

## The Revision Process

### From First Draft to Final Draft

- **Initial Review:**
  - Begin by reading your first draft aloud. This helps you hear how your vows sound and identify any awkward phrasing or areas that need improvement.
    - Example:
      - "I promise to always support you" might sound better as "I vow to stand by your side through every challenge."
- **Get Feedback:**
  - Share your first draft with a trusted friend or family member. Their feedback can provide a fresh perspective and highlight areas you might have overlooked.
    - Example:
      - "Your friend might suggest rephrasing a sentence for clarity or adding more personal anecdotes."

## Techniques for Revising and Refining

### Editing for Clarity and Impact

- **Simplify Your Language:**
  - Ensure your vows are clear and concise. Avoid overly complex sentences or jargon that might confuse your audience.
    - Example:
      - "I pledge to uphold the sanctity of our union" could be simplified to "I promise to cherish and honor our marriage."
- **Focus on Specifics:**
  - Include specific details and personal anecdotes that make your vows unique and memorable.

- **Example:**
  - "I will always love you" becomes more impactful as "I will always love you, especially when you make me laugh on a bad day."

Enhancing Emotional Resonance

- **Balance Emotion and Humor:**
  - Strive for a balance between heartfelt emotions and light-hearted moments. This can make your vows more engaging and relatable.
    - **Example:**
      - "I vow to support your dreams, and to always laugh at your jokes, even the terrible ones."
- **Show, Don't Tell:**
  - Use descriptive language to paint a picture of your feelings and promises. This creates a more vivid and emotional connection.
    - **Example:**
      - Instead of saying "I love you," describe a moment that illustrates your love, such as "I knew I loved you when you stayed up all night with me during my toughest times."

Refining Your Message

- **Take Breaks:**
  - Allow time between revisions to gain fresh perspective. Returning to your vows with a clear mind can help you identify areas for improvement.
    - Example:
      - "Take a day or two away from your vows before revisiting them for further edits."
- **Iterate and Improve:**
  - Each draft should bring you closer to your final version. Don't be afraid to make significant changes if it enhances the clarity and emotional impact of your vows.
    - Example:
      - "Rewriting an entire paragraph to better capture a shared memory or commitment."

---

Revising and polishing your wedding vows is a crucial step to ensure they are meaningful, clear, and emotionally resonant. By embracing the revision process, utilizing techniques for refining your language and emotions, and understanding the importance of multiple drafts, you can create vows that truly reflect your love and commitment. This careful attention to detail will help make your vows a cherished part of your wedding ceremony and your life together.

Getting Feedback

Seeking Opinions

Constructive feedback is invaluable when refining your wedding vows. Knowing who to ask and how to balance their advice with your own voice is essential.

Who to Ask for Constructive Feedback

- **Trusted Friends and Family:**
  - Choose individuals who know you well and understand your relationship. They can provide insights that resonate with your personal story.
- **Experienced Married Couples:**
  - Friends or family members who have written their own vows can offer practical advice and share what worked for them.
- **Wedding Officiant:**
  - Your officiant may have experience with many weddings and can provide a professional perspective on the tone and structure of your vows.
- **Professional Writers or Editors:**
  - If available, a professional writer or editor can help you refine the language and ensure clarity without altering your voice.

Balancing Advice with Your Own Voice

- **Stay True to Yourself:**
  - While feedback is helpful, it's essential to maintain your authentic voice. Your vows should reflect your feelings and personality.
- **Selective Implementation:**
  - Not all feedback needs to be implemented. Use your judgment to decide which advice resonates with you and improves your vows.
- **Maintain Emotional Integrity:**
  - Ensure that any revisions keep the emotional integrity of your vows intact. The primary goal is to convey your genuine love and commitment.

- **Multiple Drafts:**
  - Embrace the process of writing multiple drafts. Each iteration will bring you closer to a polished final version that you're proud of.
- **Practice Aloud:**
  - Regularly practice reading your vows aloud to gauge their impact and ensure they flow naturally.

---

Revising and polishing your wedding vows involves a thoughtful balance of personal reflection, constructive feedback, and multiple drafts. By seeking opinions from trusted individuals, staying true to your voice, and refining your vows through practice, you can create a powerful and heartfelt expression of your love. These carefully crafted words will resonate deeply on your wedding day and throughout your married life.

## Polishing Your Vows

The final touches on your wedding vows involve ensuring they are polished, grammatically correct, and easy to read. Attention to detail at this stage will help you deliver your vows confidently and beautifully on your wedding day.

### Grammar, Tone, and Readability

- **Grammar and Punctuation:**
  - Carefully review your vows for any grammatical errors or punctuation mistakes. Correct grammar ensures clarity and professionalism.
    - Example:
      - "Double-check the use of commas, periods, and capitalization to make sure your vows are clear and easy to understand."
- **Consistent Tone:**
  - Maintain a consistent tone throughout your vows. Whether you choose a romantic, humorous, or formal tone, consistency will make your vows more cohesive and impactful.
    - Example:
      - "If you start with a light-hearted anecdote, ensure the rest of your vows match that tone rather than switching to a very formal style."
- **Readability:**
  - Ensure your vows are easy to read aloud. Short sentences and simple language can help convey your emotions more effectively and make it easier for you to speak naturally.
    - Example:
      - "Break down long sentences into shorter ones to improve readability and delivery."

- **Proofreading:**
  - Carefully proofread your vows multiple times. Consider having someone else review them as well to catch any errors you might have missed.
    - Example:
      - "Ask a trusted friend to read through your vows for any spelling or grammatical errors."
- **Final Edits:**
  - Make any final edits necessary to improve the flow and impact of your vows. Focus on clarity, emotional resonance, and brevity.
    - Example:
      - "If a sentence feels clunky or awkward, rephrase it for smoother delivery."
- **Practice Makes Perfect:**
  - Practice reading your vows aloud multiple times. This will help you become more comfortable with the words and improve your delivery.
    - Example:
      - "Practice in front of a mirror or record yourself to fine-tune your delivery and timing."
- **Written Copy:**
  - Prepare a clean, final written copy of your vows. Consider printing them on a small card or using a nicely bound booklet to hold during the ceremony.
    - Example:
      - "Print your vows on a small card that fits easily in your hand and looks elegant."

Polishing your wedding vows involves careful attention to grammar, tone, and readability. By thoroughly proofreading, making final edits, and practicing your delivery, you can ensure your vows are polished and error-free. These final touches will help you deliver heartfelt, clear, and impactful vows on your wedding day, creating a memorable and meaningful moment for you and your partner.

# ADDITIONAL TIPS...

Writing and revising wedding vows can be an emotionally charged and creatively challenging process. Here are some additional tips to help you craft vows that feel authentic and heartfelt:

**Take Breaks Between Drafts to Gain Fresh Perspectives**

- **Allow Time to Reflect:**
  - Step away from your vows for a day or two before revisiting them. This break can help you see your words with fresh eyes and gain new insights.
    - **Example:**
      - "After writing your initial draft, take a couple of days to focus on other aspects of wedding planning before returning to revise your vows."

- **Avoid Rushing:**
  - Give yourself plenty of time to write, revise, and polish your vows. Rushed work can lead to missed errors and less impactful vows.
    - **Example:**
      - "Start writing your vows well in advance of your wedding day to ensure you have ample time for revisions."

- **Listen to Your Heart:**
  - Your vows should reflect your true feelings and intentions. Trust your instincts about what feels right and authentic for you and your partner.
    - **Example:**
      - "If a suggested change doesn't resonate with you, it's okay to stick with your original wording."
- **Personal Connection:**
  - Ensure that your vows feel personally meaningful. They should encapsulate your unique relationship and the promises you want to make to your partner.
    - **Example:**
      - "Focus on what truly matters to you and your partner, rather than trying to meet others' expectations."

Revising and polishing your wedding vows is a thoughtful and creative process that benefits from taking breaks, reading aloud, and trusting your instincts. These additional tips can help you refine your vows to ensure they are heartfelt, clear, and genuinely reflective of your love and commitment. By dedicating time and care to this process, you can create vows that will be a cherished part of your wedding day and your life together.

# Wedding Vow Examples

Writing your own wedding vows can be challenging, but seeing examples can provide inspiration and guidance. This chapter offers a variety of wedding vow examples to help you craft vows that are personal, heartfelt, and reflective of your relationship.



## CHAPTER 08

**Traditional Vows**

- **Example 1:**
    - "I, [Name], take you, [Partner's Name], to be my lawfully wedded [husband/wife], to have and to hold, from this day forward, for better, for worse, for richer, for poorer, in sickness and in health, until death do us part."
- **Example 2:**
    - "I promise to love you, comfort you, honor and keep you in sickness and in health, for richer or poorer, for better or worse, and forsaking all others, be faithful to you as long as we both shall live."
- **Example 3:**
    - "I, [Name], pledge to be your faithful partner in sickness and in health, in times of joy and sorrow. I promise to love and honor you all the days of my life."

Traditional vows often emphasize enduring commitment and fidelity, expressing timeless promises that have stood the test of time across generations and cultures.

**Romantic Vows**

- **Example 1:**
    - "From the moment our eyes met, I knew my heart had found its home. Today, I stand before you, promising to love you fiercely and faithfully. I vow to cherish our bond, to support your dreams, and to always hold your hand through life's joys and challenges."
- **Example 2:**
    - "From the first moment our paths crossed, I knew my life was forever changed. Today, I give you my heart and soul, promising to cherish you as my equal and partner in all things. With you, I am home, and together, our love will light the way through every moment of our lives."

- **Example 3:**
    - "In your eyes, I have found my truest reflection and my closest friend. I promise to cherish our bond and to celebrate our love each day. With you, I am complete."

Romantic vows are infused with heartfelt expressions of love and devotion, often weaving in poetic language and personal sentiments that reflect the unique connection between the couple.


## Personalized Vows

- **Example 1:**
    - "Remember the first time we laughed together? Today, I promise to always bring laughter into our lives. I promise to stand by your side, to support your dreams, and to love you unconditionally, just as you are."
- **Example 2:**
    - "Do you remember the first time we danced under the stars? In that moment, I knew you were my forever dance partner. Today, I vow to keep dancing through life with you, celebrating our triumphs and supporting each other in our struggles. I promise to always be your rock, your confidant, and your greatest fan."
- **Example 3:**
    - "In you, I have found my truest friend and greatest love. I promise to always listen with compassion, speak with honesty, and support your dreams as if they were my own. Today and every day, I choose you, to laugh with you in joy, to grieve with you in sorrow, and to grow with you in love."

Personalized vows reflect the couple's individual values, promises, and aspirations, showcasing their journey and commitment to each other's happiness.

Humorous Vows

- **Example 1:**
  - "I promise to always be your partner in crime, your fellow adventurer, and your favorite person to annoy. I vow to keep our fridge stocked with snacks and to laugh with you, even when we're old and wrinkly."
- **Example 2:**
  - "I vow to be your partner in adventure, your co-conspirator in mischief, and your ally in all things. I promise to laugh at your jokes, even the ones that aren't funny, and to always share my popcorn at the movies. Let's face life's challenges together with laughter and love, knowing that together, we can conquer anything."

Humorous vows infuse light-heartedness and joy into the ceremony, highlighting the couple's shared sense of humor and playful spirit.


Creative Vows

- **Example 1:**
  - "With this ring, I give you my heart. Just as it encircles your finger, so will my love forever encircle your heart. I pledge my life and my love to you, promising to be your partner in all things, from this day forward."
- **Example 2:**
  - "With each beat of my heart, I promise to love you deeper than the oceans and higher than the mountains. I vow to write our story together with words of kindness, compassion, and respect. Today, I give you not just my hand and my heart, but my soul, knowing that our love will be our greatest adventure."
- **Example 3:**
  - "In the garden of life, I promise to be your sunshine, nourishing our love with laughter, patience, and kindness. I vow to cherish our moments together and to nurture our bond with tenderness and grace."

Creative vows use poetic language and symbolic gestures to convey the depth and passion of the couple's love, expressing their unique bond in a memorable and meaningful way.

Inspirational Vows

- **Example 1:**
  - "Today, I stand before you, ready to embark on the greatest journey of our lives. I promise to be your unwavering support, your partner in dreaming big, and your refuge in times of uncertainty. Together, let's create a legacy of love, kindness, and courage, inspiring each other to reach new heights and embrace every moment with gratitude."
- **Example 2:**
  - "Today, I promise to be your strength when you feel weak, your cheerleader in times of triumph, and your partner in all of life's adventures. Together, let's build a future filled with love, laughter, and endless possibilities."
- **Example 3:**
  - "I promise to be your partner in dreaming big and your comfort in times of uncertainty. Together, let's embrace every adventure with courage and gratitude, knowing that with love, we can achieve anything."

Inspirational vows inspire hope and optimism for the future, expressing a shared vision of growth, support, and mutual respect as the couple embarks on their journey together.

These examples illustrate the diversity of wedding vows and demonstrate how you can personalize your vows to reflect your unique relationship and personalities. Whether you draw inspiration from traditional, romantic, humorous, creative, or inspirational themes, the essence of meaningful vows lies in their sincerity and alignment with your shared values. Use these examples as a starting point to craft vows that celebrate your love and commitment on your wedding day, creating a heartfelt and memorable ceremony for you and your partner.